The Essential Rosary

Also published by
Sophia Institute Press:

Wood of the Cradle, Wood of the Cross:
The Little Way of the Infant Jesus
by Caryll Houselander

The Essential Rosary

with prayers by
Caryll Houselander

SOPHIA INSTITUTE PRESS®
Manchester, New Hampshire

The prayers by Caryll Houselander in this book originally appeared in Maisie Ward's *The Splendor of the Rosary*, published by Sheed & Ward in New York in 1945.

Copyright ©1996 Sophia Institute Press
All rights reserved
Cover design by Joan Barger

The cover painting is "Madonna and Child" by Bernardino Pinturicchio from the Vatican Museum (Scala/Art Resource, New York).

Sophia Institute Press
Box 5284, Manchester NH 03108
1-800-888-9344

Library of Congress Cataloging-in-Publication Data

Houselander, Caryll.
    The essential rosary / with prayers by Caryll Houselander.
        p. cm.
    ISBN 0-918477-36-0 (pbk. : alk. paper)
    1. Mysteries of the Rosary.   I. Title.
BX2163.H68   1996   95-50280
242' .74—dc20   CIP

97 98 99 10 9 8 7 6 5 4

Contents

Editor's Note

The biblical references in the following pages
are based on the Douay-Rheims edition
of the Old and New Testaments.

The texts of the *Our Father,* the *Apostles' Creed,*
and the *Hail Mary* are taken from the
Catechism of the Catholic Church.

The Essential Rosary

Introduction

German bombs were raining down on war-time London when Caryll Houselander composed the Rosary prayers contained in this book. In a letter to Maisie Ward, who had commissioned these prayers for Ward's book *The Splendor of the Rosary,* Houselander wrote:

> All these were written in shelters or, if not in shelters, in pauses during work forced on me by the bombs. It was only the Doodles[1] going actually overhead which enabled me to do them, and I was strangely sure of just one thing, that the things I was praying *for* were the essential things, the things which are so much more real and lasting than destruction and folly and fear....[2]

The Rosary is a prayer for and about essential things. It is composed of the most basic prayers of the Catholic faith — the *Apostles' Creed,* the *Lord's Prayer,* the *Hail Mary,* and the *Glory Be.* Its Mysteries focus on the central events of the Gospel as recorded in Scripture: Christ's

---

[1] Doodlebugs: a type of German bomb used during World War II.
[2] Maisie Ward, *The Splendor of the Rosary* (New York: Sheed and Ward, 1945), 6.

birth, His Passion, and His Resurrection. These events, in turn, are seen through the eyes of the one who was in many ways the first — and in that sense, the most essential — disciple: Mary, the mother of Jesus.

Given that it is a simple prayer based on essentials, there is no wonder that the Rosary is so popular and is prayed by Catholics of all ages, backgrounds, and cultures. In many ways, the Rosary is like the Mass. Its basic format is simple and fixed, and yet admits of great elaboration and variation in its details to meet specific situations and the concerns of those who pray it. From this come the endless variations of Rosary prayers described in books and pamphlets — the addition of petitions, invocations, intentions, and so forth.

Knowing this, we add one element to the essential Rosary presented in this book — prayers by Caryll Houselander. Houselander was a modern-day English Catholic mystic whose spiritual writings combine a sure grasp of Catholic dogma, a sacramental vision of the natural world's beauty, and a shrewd, often humorous insight into human nature.

These prayers are a wonderful introduction to the characteristic features of Houselander's thought: her lyrical imagery, her intense identification with Christ, her conviction that He is present in all persons, and her deep devotion to the Eucharist.

More importantly, through these prayers, House-lander shows us that meditation on the Mysteries of the

Rosary is not simply an intellectual exercise. Rather, the Rosary can and should help us to live out our Christian discipleship in our everyday existence by placing before our minds the fundamental virtues, exemplified by our Lord and His mother, which all Christians must strive to imitate: humility, obedience, patience, and charity.

This is something which you can only learn through experience. In the end, all that a Rosary book can do is guide and encourage you. The true, essential fruits of the Rosary come only to those who pray it sincerely.

It is therefore our hope that you will read the instructions in this book, reflect on its prayers, and then simply pray the Rosary yourself. Only then will you enjoy the consolation and wisdom this time-honored prayer offers to all those who embrace its simple discipline.

❧❧❧❧❧

How to Pray the Rosary

The complete Rosary consists of fifteen decades, including all three sets of Mysteries, beginning with the five Joyful Mysteries, continuing through the five Sorrowful Mysteries, and concluding with the five Glorious Mysteries.

Most people pray only five decades of the Rosary on any given day: the Joyful Mysteries on Mondays and Thursdays, the Sorrowful Mysteries on Tuesdays and Fridays, and the Glorious Mysteries on Wednesdays, Saturdays, and Sundays.

It is customary to announce the name of the Mystery you are praying before beginning to recite the prayers that accompany its meditation.

We have placed at the beginning of each Mystery a biblical passage and at the end a prayer by Caryll Houselander. You may omit these if you choose to pray only the essential Rosary, or, as an aid to your meditation, include them—silently or aloud—in the order in which we have placed them.

The diagram on the following page shows the sequence of prayers said in each decade and the bead that you should hold as you say each prayer. The prayers themselves are found at the end of this book.

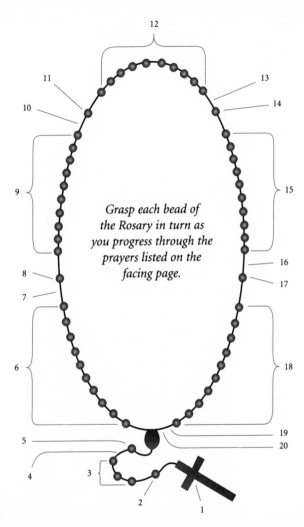

Grasp each bead of the Rosary in turn as you progress through the prayers listed on the facing page.

How to Pray the Rosary

1. Make the *Sign of the Cross* and say the *Apostles' Creed.*

2. Say the *Our Father.*

3. Say three *Hail Marys.*

4. Say the *Glory Be* and the *O My Jesus.*

5. Announce the first Mystery, and say the *Our Father.*

6. Say ten *Hail Marys.*

7. Say the *Glory Be* and the *O My Jesus.*

8. Announce the second Mystery, and say the *Our Father.*

9. Say ten *Hail Marys.*

10. Say the *Glory Be* and the *O My Jesus.*

11. Announce the third Mystery, and say the *Our Father.*

12. Say ten *Hail Marys.*

13. Say the *Glory Be* and the *O My Jesus.*

14. Announce the fourth Mystery, and say the *Our Father.*

15. Say ten *Hail Marys.*

16. Say the *Glory Be* and the *O My Jesus.*

17. Announce the fifth Mystery, and say the *Our Father.*

18. Say ten *Hail Marys.*

19. Say the *Glory Be* and the *O My Jesus.*

20. Now either begin the next set of Mysteries at 5 (above) or conclude this Rosary with the *Hail, Holy Queen,* the *Invocation,* and the *Sign of the Cross.*

Praying the Rosary

Beginning Prayers of the Rosary

(Prayed every day)

Take the cross at the end of the string of beads
into your hand. Make the Sign of the Cross:

In the name of the Father,
and of the Son,
and of the Holy Spirit.
Amen.

৪৹৪৹৪৹

Now recite the Apostles' Creed:

I believe in God, the Father almighty,
creator of Heaven and earth.
I believe in Jesus Christ,
His only Son, our Lord.
He was conceived
by the power of the Holy Spirit
and born of the Virgin Mary.
He suffered under Pontius Pilate,
was crucified, died, and was buried.
He descended into Hell.
On the third day He rose again.
He ascended into Heaven and
is seated at the right hand of the Father.
He will come again to judge
the living and the dead.
I believe in the Holy Spirit,
the holy Catholic Church,
the Communion of Saints,
the forgiveness of sins,
the resurrection of the body,
and the life everlasting.
Amen.

❧❧❧❧❧

Moving to the next single bead,
say the Our Father:

Our Father who art in Heaven,
hallowed be Thy name.
Thy kingdom come.
Thy will be done on earth,
as it is in Heaven.
Give us this day our daily bread,
and forgive us our trespasses,
as we forgive those who trespass against us,
and lead us not into temptation,
but deliver us from evil.
Amen.

෨෧෨෧෨෧

On each of the next three beads,
recite the Hail Mary:

Hail Mary, full of grace,
the Lord is with thee;
blessed art thou among women,
and blessed is the
fruit of thy womb, Jesus.
Holy Mary, Mother of God,
pray for us sinners,
now and at the hour of our death.
Amen.

ഇഇഇഇ

Recite the Glory Be:

Glory be to the Father,
and to the Son,
and to the Holy Spirit;
as it was in the beginning,
is now, and ever shall be,
world without end.
Amen.

❧❧❧❧❧

Recite the O My Jesus:

O my Jesus,
forgive us our sins,
save us from the fires of Hell.
Lead all souls to Heaven,
especially those who have
most need of Thy mercy.
Amen.

ଓଉଓଉଓଉ

The Joyful Mysteries
(Prayed Mondays and Thursdays)

The First Joyful Mystery

છ૦:છ૦:છ૦:

The Annunciation

And the angel answering, said to Mary: "The Holy Spirit shall come upon thee, and the power of the most High shall overshadow thee. And therefore also the Holy One which shall be born of thee shall be called the Son of God."

Luke 1:35

છ૦:છ૦:

–one–
Our Father, who art in Heaven . . .

–ten–
Hail Mary, full of grace . . .

–one–
Glory be to the Father . . .

–one–
O my Jesus . . .

Prayer

Descend,
    Holy Spirit of Life!
    Come down into our hearts,
    that we may live.

Descend into emptiness,
    that emptiness
    may be filled.

Descend into the dust,
    that the dust may flower.

Descend into the dark,
    that the light
    may shine in darkness.

ಶಿಶಿಶಿ

ଚ୍ଚ‍ଚ‍ଚ‍ଚ‍ଚ

The Visitation

When Elizabeth heard the salutation
of Mary, the infant leaped in her
womb. And Elizabeth was filled with
the Holy Spirit, and she cried out with
a loud voice, and said: "Blessed art thou
among women, and blessed
is the fruit of thy womb."

Luke 1:41-42

ଚ‍ଚ‍ଚ‍ଚ

–one–
Our Father, who art in Heaven . . .

–ten–
Hail Mary, full of grace . . .

–one–
Glory be to the Father . . .

–one–
O my Jesus . . .

Prayer

Breath of Heaven,
   carry us on the impulse
  of Christ's love,
    as easily as thistledown
    is carried on the wind;
that in the Advent season of our souls,
   while He is formed in us,
    in secret and in silence—
the Creator
   in the hands of His creatures,
    as the Host
    in the hands of the priest—
we may carry Him forth
   to wherever He wishes to be,
    as Mary carried Him over the hills
    on His errand of love,
   to the house of Elizabeth.

❧❧❧❧❧

ଚ୍ଚ:ଚ୍ଚ:ଚ୍ଚ

The Nativity

And it came to pass that when they were there, her days were accomplished that she should be delivered. And she brought forth her firstborn son, and wrapped Him up in swaddling clothes, and laid Him in a manger, because there was no room for them in the inn.

Luke 2:6-7

ଚ୍ଚ:ଚ୍ଚ

–one–
Our Father, who art in Heaven . . .

–ten–
Hail Mary, full of grace . . .

–one–
Glory be to the Father . . .

–one–
O my Jesus . . .

Prayer

Be born in us,
  Incarnate Love.

Take our flesh and blood,
  and give us Your humanity;

Take our eyes,
  and give us Your vision;

Take our minds,
  and give us Your pure thought;

Take our feet,
  and set them in Your path;

Take our hands,
  and fold them in Your prayer;

Take our hearts,
  and give them Your will to love.

❧❧❧❧

The Fourth Joyful Mystery

☙☙☙☙☙☙

The Presentation

And after the days of her purification
were accomplished, they carried Him to
Jerusalem, to present Him to the Lord,
and to offer a sacrifice, according as it is
written in the law of the Lord, a pair of
turtledoves or two young pigeons.

Luke 2:22-24

☙☙☙☙

–one–
Our Father, who art in Heaven . . .

–ten–
Hail Mary, full of grace . . .

–one–
Glory be to the Father . . .

–one–
O my Jesus . . .

Prayer

By the humility
of Jesus, Mary, and Joseph,
    give us the glory of humility.

By the mystery
of innocence
obeying the law
binding upon sinners,
    make us obedient.

By the offering of the poor,
the two white doves
in the gentle hands
of the pure Mother of Love,
    give us the spirit of poverty.

❧❧❧❧❧

The Fifth Joyful Mystery

❦❧❦❧❦❧

The Finding in the Temple

And having fulfilled the days, when they returned,
the child Jesus remained in Jerusalem, and His
parents knew it not. And not finding Him, they
returned into Jerusalem, seeking Him. And it came
to pass that, after three days, they found Him in
the Temple, sitting in the midst of the doctors,
hearing them and asking them questions.

Luke 2:43-46

❦❧❦❧

–one–
Our Father, who art in Heaven . . .

–ten–
Hail Mary, full of grace . . .

–one–
Glory be to the Father . . .

–one–
O my Jesus . . .

Prayer

Through Mary,
seeking her lost son,
    may we be given grace
    always to seek for the Christ-child
    and always to find Him.

Let us find Him in all children,
and in all who have a child's needs—
    the helpless, the sick,
    the simple, the aged;
    in all who serve
    and are trusting and poor;
    in all who are lonely or homeless.

Let us, too, become as little children,
    to find the Divine Child
    in our own hearts.

❧❧❧❧

If you are saying the entire
fifteen-decade Rosary, proceed
to the Sorrowful Mysteries.

To conclude your recitation
of the Rosary with this Mystery,
turn to page 61.

❧❧❧❧❧❧

The Sorrowful Mysteries
(Prayed Tuesdays and Fridays)

ভাৎভাৎভাৎ

The Agony in the Garden

And He was withdrawn away from them a
stone's cast. And kneeling down, He prayed,
saying: "Father, if Thou wilt, remove this
chalice from me; but yet not my will but
Thine be done." And there appeared to Him
an angel from Heaven, strengthening Him.
And being in an agony, He prayed the longer.

Luke 22:41-43

ভাৎভাৎ

—one—
Our Father, who art in Heaven . . .

—ten—
Hail Mary, full of grace . . .

—one—
Glory be to the Father . . .

—one—
O my Jesus . . .

Prayer

By Your heaviness and fear
    in Gethsemane,
  comfort the oppressed
    and those who are afraid.

By Your loneliness,
  facing the Passion
    while the Apostles slept,
  comfort those who face evil alone
    while the world sleeps.

By Your persistent prayer,
    in anguish of anticipation,
  strengthen those
    who shrink from the unknown.

By Your humility,
    taking the comfort of angels,
  give us grace to help
    and to be helped by each other,
  and in each other
    to comfort You,
      Jesus Christ.

❧❧❧

The Second Sorrowful Mystery

ଊଊଊଊ

The Scourging
at the Pillar

Then, therefore, Pilate took Jesus
and scourged Him.

John 19:1

ଊଊଊ

–one–
Our Father, who art in Heaven . . .

–ten–
Hail Mary, full of grace . . .

–one–
Glory be to the Father . . .

–one–
O my Jesus . . .

Prayer

Lord,
mocked, and scourged at the pillar,
    when Pilate made his pitiful effort
    to compromise,
        by scourging Innocence.

Christ, so gentle to the
    weakness and folly of men,
        make us patient
            with the lash and whip
                of circumstance,
            with the bruising of life,
                the thong for our own shoulders,
                    made by our own weakness,
                    malice, and stupidity.

Help us to accept it
    as our just due,
not complaining,
    but with the dignity
    and humility
        of Your imperious will.

❧❧❧❧❧

The Third Sorrowful Mystery

ഊഃഊഃഊഃ

The Crowning with Thorns

Then the soldiers of the governor, taking Jesus
into the hall, gathered unto Him the whole band.
And stripping Him, they put a scarlet cloak about
Him. And plaiting a crown of thorns, they put it
upon His head, and a reed in His right hand.
And bowing the knee before Him, they mocked
Him, saying: "Hail, King of the Jews."

Matthew 27:27-29

ഊഃഊഃ

–one–
Our Father, who art in Heaven . . .

–ten–
Hail Mary, full of grace . . .

–one–
Glory be to the Father . . .

–one–
O my Jesus . . .

Prayer

Christ crowned with thorns,
give us courage to think,
to sift and measure and weigh;
to wrestle with the angel,
and if needs be,
to enter into darkness,
disillusion, and doubt,
in the search for truth.

Illumine our minds,
though our eyes be blinded
by Your bright ray.

Crown us, Your servants,
with the only crown fitting
for vassals of the Lord of Light;
crown us, Lord,
with Your crown of thorns.

ဢၚၩၚ

The Carrying of the Cross

And bearing His own Cross, Jesus went forth
to that place which is called *Calvary,*
but in Hebrew, *Golgotha.*

John 19:17

And they forced a passerby coming out
of the country, Simon the Cyrenian (the father
of Alexander and Rufus), to take up His Cross.

Mark 15:21

ဢၚၚ

–one–
Our Father, who art in Heaven . . .

–ten–
Hail Mary, full of grace . . .

–one–
Glory be to the Father . . .

–one–
O my Jesus . . .

Prayer

Lord, let us take up the cross;
it is the heavy load of our sins—
    our pride and materialism and greed.

We all share the responsibility
    of lifting it from the backs
        of the innocents
            who are crushed under it.

Let our communion with You,
    and with one another,
be proved by our will to suffer,
    so that all our hands,
        lifting the bitter wood together,
            may lighten it for each other
    and each of us
        may be a Cyrenian to You,
            Christ, through the ages
            bearing our cross.

ༀༀༀༀ

The Fifth Sorrowful Mystery

꧁꧂꧁꧂꧁꧂

The Crucifixion

And it was the third hour,
and they crucified Him.

Mark 15:25

With Christ I am nailed to the Cross.

Galatians 2:19

꧁꧂꧁꧂꧁꧂

–one–
Our Father, who art in Heaven . . .

–ten–
Hail Mary, full of grace . . .

–one–
Glory be to the Father . . .

–one–
O my Jesus . . .

Prayer

Nail our hands
in Your hands
to the Cross.

Make us take and hold
the hard thing.

Nail our feet
in Your feet
to the Cross,
that they may never
wander away from You.

Make our promises and our vows,
nails that hold us fast,
that even our dead weight of sin,
dragging on the nails
in our last weakness,
may not separate us from You,
but may make us one with You
in Your redeeming love.

❧❧❧❧❧

*If you are saying the entire
fifteen-decade Rosary, proceed
to the Glorious Mysteries.*

*To conclude your recitation
of the Rosary with this Mystery,
turn to page 61.*

෧෧෧෧෧

The Glorious Mysteries

(Prayed Wednesdays, Saturdays, and Sundays)

The First Glorious Mystery

ʘʘʘʘʘ

The Resurrection

And the angel answering, said to the women:
"Fear not, for I know that you seek Jesus
who was crucified. He is not here, for
He is risen, as He said. Come and see
the place where the Lord was laid."

Matthew 28:5-6

ʘʘʘʘ

–one–
Our Father, who art in Heaven . . .

–ten–
Hail Mary, full of grace . . .

–one–
Glory be to the Father . . .

–one–
O my Jesus . . .

Prayer

Seed of Eternal Life,
  sown by love's flowering
    in the heavy clay of our hearts,
  rise in us;
    be our soul's spring.

By the risen feet of Christ,
  walking upon the delicate grass;
by the wakened hands of Christ,
  touching the cool petals of flowers;
by the opened eyes of Christ,
  looking with joy
    on all created things;
teach us to wonder,
  and to walk upon the earth
    aware of earth's loveliness,
    aware of the Being of God
      in all that is.

❧❧❧❧❧

The Second Glorious Mystery

⊙⊙⊙⊙⊙

The Ascension

And when Jesus had said these things,
while they looked on, He was
raised up, and a cloud received
Him out of their sight.

Acts 1:9

⊙⊙⊙

—one—
Our Father, who art in Heaven . . .

—ten—
Hail Mary, full of grace . . .

—one—
Glory be to the Father . . .

—one—
O my Jesus . . .

Prayer

Christ,
  ascended into Heaven,
You bear the wounds
  of the whole world
  in Your hands and feet
  and in Your heart.

They plead for us,
  shining like stars
    before the secret face of God.

By Your five wounds
  purify our five senses;
  lift up our hearts into Heaven.

While You draw down
God's mercy to us,
    showing our wounds
    in Your glorified Body,
let us draw men up to You,
    showing Your wounds to the world,
    scored on our grey dust
    in the bright crimson
        of Your love.

❧❧❧❧❧❧

The Third Glorious Mystery

ꙮꙮꙮ

The Descent of the Holy Spirit

And suddenly there came a sound from Heaven
as of a mighty wind coming, and it filled the
whole house where they were sitting. And there
appeared to them parted tongues, as it were of
fire, and it sat upon every one of them. And
they were all filled with the Holy Spirit.

Acts 2:2-4

ꙮꙮ

–one–
Our Father, who art in Heaven . . .

–ten–
Hail Mary, full of grace . . .

–one–
Glory be to the Father . . .

–one–
O my Jesus . . .

Prayer

Come down upon us,
  Spirit of God,
  Spirit of wisdom and peace and joy;
come as a great wind blowing;
  sweep our minds with a storm of light.

Be in us as bright fire burning;
  forge our wills to shining swords
    in the flame.

Purify our hearts
  in the crucible of the fire of love.

Change our tepid nature
  into the warm humanity of Christ,
    as He changed water to wine.

Be in us a stream of life,
  as wine in the living vine.

The Fourth Glorious Mystery

ରେଡ଼ର

The Assumption

My soul doth magnify the Lord, and my
spirit hath rejoiced in God my Savior.
Because He hath regarded the humility of
His handmaid; for behold from henceforth
all generations shall call me blessed.

Luke 1:46-48

ରେଡ଼

–one–
Our Father, who art in Heaven . . .

–ten–
Hail Mary, full of grace . . .

–one–
Glory be to the Father . . .

–one–
O my Jesus . . .

Prayer

Mother of Christ,
*   we rejoice in you,*
*   created to be the wheat*
*   for the Bread of Life.*

When the dark winds and the rain
*   drove the harvest field*
*   to a storm of gold,*
locked in His love
you were unique to God
*   among the multitudinous wheat,*
*   the chosen grain for the Host.*

Now, the red sheaves are bound,
*   the grain sifted and threshed,*
*   the wheat in the bread.*

Now, the Creator's hands
*   that sheltered you,*
*   like a fended flame in the wind,*
reach down from a Heaven
*   of cloudless blue,*
receiving you into eternal light.

ᙣᙍᙣᙍᙣ

The Fifth Glorious Mystery

❦❦❦❦❦❦

The Coronation of
the Blessed Virgin

And a great sign appeared in Heaven:
a woman clothed with the sun, and
the moon under her feet, and on her
head a crown of twelve stars.

Revelation 12:1

❦❦❦❦

—one—
Our Father, who art in Heaven . . .

—ten—
Hail Mary, full of grace . . .

—one—
Glory be to the Father . . .

—one—
O my Jesus . . .

Prayer

Mary,
Immaculate Love,
  we bless you.

Because, though rooted in earth
  as we are,
you opened your heart to God;
  expanding and opening wide
  to the heat of the sun
  in your sinless heart,
you opened our hearts
  to the light.

All generations bless you,
flower of our race.

We are crowned
  in you,
Queen of Heaven,
  crowned with stars
  by the hands of Christ.

*To conclude your recitation
of the Rosary with this Mystery,
go to the next page.*

❧❧❧❧❧

Concluding Prayers
of the Rosary
(Prayed every day)

Say the Hail, Holy Queen:

Hail, Holy Queen, Mother of Mercy!
Our life, our sweetness, and our hope!
To thee do we cry,
poor banished children of Eve;
to thee do we send up our sighs,
mourning and weeping
in this valley of tears.
Turn, then, most gracious advocate,
thine eyes of mercy toward us;
and after this our exile show unto us
the blessed fruit of thy womb, Jesus.
O clement, O loving,
O sweet Virgin Mary!
Pray for us, O holy Mother of God,
that we may be made worthy
of the promises of Christ.
Amen.

❧❧❧❧❧

Then recite the Invocation:

O God, whose only-begotten Son,
by His life, death, and Resurrection,
has purchased for us
the rewards of eternal life,
grant, we beseech Thee,
that meditating on these Mysteries
of the most holy Rosary
of the Blessed Virgin Mary,
we may imitate what they contain,
and obtain what they promise,
through the same Christ our Lord.
Amen.

*Conclude your recitation of the Rosary
with the Sign of the Cross:*

In the name of the Father,
and of the Son,
and of the Holy Spirit.
Amen.

The Prayers of the Rosary
(Listed alphabetically)

Apostles' Creed

I believe in God, the Father almighty, creator of Heaven and earth.

I believe in Jesus Christ, His only Son, our Lord. He was conceived by the power of the Holy Spirit and born of the Virgin Mary. He suffered under Pontius Pilate, was crucified, died, and was buried.

He descended into Hell. On the third day He rose again. He ascended into Heaven and is seated at the right hand of the Father. He will come again to judge the living and the dead.

I believe in the Holy Spirit, the holy Catholic Church, the Communion of Saints, the forgiveness of sins, the resurrection of the body, and the life everlasting. Amen.

Glory Be

Glory be to the Father, and to the Son, and to the Holy Spirit; as it was in the beginning, is now, and ever shall be, world without end. Amen.

Hail, Holy Queen

Hail, Holy Queen, Mother of Mercy! Our life, our sweetness, and our hope! To thee do we cry, poor banished children of Eve; to thee do we send up our sighs, mourning and weeping in this valley of tears. Turn, then, most gracious advocate, thine eyes of mercy toward us; and after this our exile show unto us the blessed fruit of thy womb, Jesus. O clement, O loving, O sweet Virgin Mary! Pray for us, O holy Mother of God, that we may be made worthy of the promises of Christ. Amen.

Hail Mary

Hail Mary, full of grace, the Lord is with thee; blessed art thou among women, and blessed is the fruit of thy womb, Jesus. Holy Mary, Mother of God, pray for us sinners, now and at the hour of our death. Amen.

Invocation

O God, whose only-begotten Son, by His life, death, and Resurrection, has purchased for us the rewards of eternal life, grant, we beseech Thee, that meditating on these Mysteries of the most holy Rosary of the Blessed Virgin Mary, we may imitate what they contain, and obtain what they promise, through the same Christ our Lord. Amen.

O My Jesus

This prayer takes its origin from the apparition of the Blessed Mother in Fatima, Portugal, in 1917, to three peasant children.

O my Jesus, forgive us our sins, save us from the fires of Hell. Lead all souls to Heaven, especially those who have most need of Thy mercy. Amen.

Our Father

Our Father who art in Heaven, hallowed be Thy name. Thy kingdom come. Thy will be done on earth, as it is in Heaven. Give us this day our daily bread, and forgive us our trespasses, as we forgive those who trespass against us, and lead us not into temptation, but deliver us from evil. Amen.

Sign of the Cross

In the name of the Father, and of the Son,
and of the Holy Spirit. Amen.

Biographical Note

Caryll Houselander
(1901-1954)

Frances Caryll Houselander was born in Bath, England, in 1901. After her mother's conversion she was baptized a Catholic with her sister in 1907.

Houselander's parents separated when she was nine, after which she was sent to convent schools until she was sixteen. A combination of personal misfortunes around this time led her to abandon the practice of Catholicism for several years.

During these years, Houselander attended St. John's Wood Art School in London, worked at a wide variety of menial jobs, and explored many different religions. By the mid-1920s, Houselander had returned to the Church and was employed as a painter and woodcarver by an ecclesiastical decorating firm.

Houselander's writing career began in the late 1920s when her spiritual director encouraged her to submit articles and drawings to *The Children's Messenger,* a religious magazine for children. After publishing her first book, *This War Is the Passion,* in 1941, Houselander continued to publish a steady stream of books up until her premature death from breast cancer in 1954. Among Houselander's most popular books are *A Rocking-Horse Catholic* and *The Reed of God.*

An ascetic who delighted both in the beauty of the English countryside and the excitement of big-city London, a Catholic laywoman longing for marriage and children who nevertheless devoted herself completely to the service of the Church, Houselander was also a mystic who saw the suffering and risen Christ in all persons regardless of their gender, race, class, or religious affiliation. She was an important twentieth-century exponent of the doctrine of the Mystical Body of Christ, which had been promulgated anew in her lifetime through Pope Pius XII's encyclical *Mystici Corporis* in 1943.

Caryll Houselander's writing—by turns comically down-to-earth and passionately ecstatic—will deepen the love of all Christians for our Lord Jesus Christ and inspire their imitation of Him in lives of sacrifice and joyful service.

๑๑๑๑๑๑

Sophia Institute Press

Sophia Institute Press

S ophia Institute is a nonprofit institution that seeks to restore man's knowledge of eternal truth, including man's knowledge of his own nature, his relation to other persons, and his relation to God.

Sophia Institute Press serves this end in numerous ways. It publishes translations of foreign works to make them accessible for the first time to English-speaking readers. It brings back into print books that have been long out of print. And it publishes important new books that fulfill the ideals of Sophia Institute. These books afford readers a rich source of the enduring wisdom of mankind.

Sophia Institute Press makes high-quality books available to the general public by using advanced technology and by soliciting donations to subsidize our general publishing costs.

Your generosity can help us provide the public with editions of works containing the enduring wisdom of the ages. Please send your tax-deductible contribution to the address below.

The members of the Editorial Board of Sophia Institute Press welcome questions, comments, and suggestions from all our readers.

For your free catalog, call:
Toll-free: 1-800-888-9344

or write:

Sophia Institute Press
Box 5284
Manchester, NH 03108

Sophia Institute is a tax-exempt institution
as defined by the Internal Revenue Code,
Section 501(c)(3). Tax I.D. 22-2548708

— My Favorite Prayers & Special Intentions —

— My Favorite Prayers & Special Intentions —

— My Favorite Prayers & Special Intentions —

— My Favorite Prayers & Special Intentions —

— My Favorite Prayers & Special Intentions —

— My Favorite Prayers & Special Intentions —

— My Favorite Prayers & Special Intentions —

— My Favorite Prayers & Special Intentions —